Beyond Sight and Touch
Indelible Realities

Philip Goggin

Grosvenor House
Publishing Limited

The right of Philip Goggin to be identified as the author of this
work has been asserted in accordance with Section 78
of the Copyright, Designs and Patents Act 1988

The book cover is copyright to Philip Goggin

This book is published by
Grosvenor House Publishing Ltd
Link House
140 The Broadway, Tolworth, Surrey, KT6 7HT.
www.grosvenorhousepublishing.co.uk

A CIP record for this book
is available from the British Library

ISBN 978-1-80381-773-6
eBook ISBN 978-1-80381-774-3

Philosophies fall away like sand, and creeds follow one another like the withered leaves of autumn; but what is beautiful is a joy for all seasons and a possession for all eternity.

—OSCAR WILDE

Preface

If you have ever wondered if events or places or experiences or people can have an existence beyond what you can see or touch, this book will be of interest to you. Even if you are a very down-to-earth person who is only concerned with what can be measured or proved, you will find here ideas which will challenge you.

But this book is not about supposed supernatural or psychic phenomena, though some claimed psychic phenomena – such as telepathy or out-of-body experiences – may be consistent with the model of the world presented here, and both lend support to it, and derive some support from it. Nor is it religious, though again its conclusions are not inconsistent with some of the teachings of mainstream religious thinkers. Nor is it a motivational guide to build self-esteem or offer possible strategies and exercises — such as meditation or the use of self-affirmations — for achieving positive outcomes.

Instead it offers ideas which can help you think of life events in new life-enhancing ways. You will be encouraged to think 'outside the box' and to appreciate the lasting impact of what you see and hear and do. If you are grieving for a lost loved one you will find new hope and comfort. If you are anxious or depressed you may find new strategies for managing your life and moving forward with new purpose.

Over the years I have been close to many people who have experienced losses of various kinds – losses of loved ones, pets, lifestyles, or possessions. All of them can count as bereavements.

I have conducted many funerals, both in a religious and non-religious setting, and had close associations with family members both before and after the event. I have benefitted from attending bereavement counselling courses (though I do not present myself as a bereavement counsellor).

In my experience of speaking with people who have gone through a bereavement I have found it helpful to emphasise the continuities of life: the way each life or event can create an echo which continues in some form. However ordinary or mundane a life or event may seem it is not without lasting significance. The same is the case with places or objects.

Over time I have mapped out ideas for understanding these processes better, drawing upon a range of philosophical, psychological and in some cases scientific insights. However, the main approach is an appeal to ordinary everyday experience and thoughtful common sense. Inevitably, as with most things to do with human experience, much is open to debate.

Uncertainty and speculation don't work for everybody. In an effort to demystify and simplify, some commentators will try to reduce our thinking and experience to something purely physical and mechanical. Typically they might say that what we call our mind is reducible to the biology of our brain. In other words, MIND=BRAIN.

That position, though held by many highly intelligent and well-read people, is not the stance taken here. Rather, the claim is that there is an invisible world of concepts, thoughts and ideas which is just as real – perhaps more real – than anything we can see or touch. That world seems to have staying power. It is not subject to the time-governed rules of the physical world. It is a world of indelible realities.

Contents

Introduction

Abstractions: what are they?

There are entities like numbers or ideas which don't have a physical existence. You could find millions of actual figures '7' written on pieces of paper, but where would you find the idea or concept of 7 or sevenness? You could find plenty of examples of anger in the world, but where would you find anger itself? These are examples of abstractions and there are many of them. Potentially an infinite number.

We use these abstractions so freely that their existence is taken for granted. We might say they are matters of common sense. For example, if you are a petrol head you will talk about abstractions like speed, acceleration, safety, reliability, cost and so. Of course you will be interested in *particular* speeds or acceleration times for any given vehicle, but you will draw upon shared concepts or abstractions in your discussion. If you are an economist you will draw upon public abstractions like inflation or interest rate as you focus on particular figures for inflation or interest rates for certain months.

Let's consider some further illustrations to show how pervasive abstractions are. Schools are to an extent judged in the UK by OFSTED (Office for Standards in Education) on their *ethos*. But where is the ethos? Can you touch it? Can you see it? An OFSTED inspector may point to aspects of pupil behaviour or the attractiveness of wall displays, or extent of parental involvement, and so on, but these are only *indicators* of ethos. The ethos itself is an abstraction. But that doesn't stop it being a reality and taken seriously by schools and inspectors.

We hear mention endlessly about the weather. But where is the weather? We can see rain or sun on a particular day, but where is 'the weather'?

Abstractions such as these are in contrast to hard physical realities like chairs or tables. These can be touched and measured in various ways. A chair occupies a certain physical space. You can smash a chair or a table. But try smashing an abstraction! Other familiar features of life may seem to be both abstract *and* concrete. For example, a school is not just a building. It is also a place where young people go with the supposed intention of learning. If a school building becomes a second-hand furniture warehouse is it still a school? Probably not. Why? Because it no longer fits the normal concept/abstraction of a school.

Leaving aside such curiosities, you may wonder *where* or *how* abstractions can exist if you can't touch them or locate them. You would be in good company in your questioning! People have puzzled over these questions down the centuries. But the bottom line as we have seen is that we speak every day in ways which presume their existence.

There is a timelessness to all of these. Some abstractions seem to have been around forever, even before there were any people to think about them, and they would seem to have an infinite future life. The concept of 7 would be an example. It's impossible to imagine how there could be a world or universe without 'sevenness'.

Other things seem to depend on human thought processes – such as 'the weather', 'anger', 'democracy', 'the monarchy' or 'humility'. It's harder to say they have always been around, because humans haven't always been around to think about them. But does that matter? They could have been waiting as it were for humans to conceptualise them, and they might continue to exist in the same way when/if there were no humans left.

Overlapping with the abstractions we have considered so far will be those unseen principles which constrain, or enable, our living as persons in the world. Here we will call these principles "powers". If you think about it, invisible powers are all around us. Obvious examples which have scientific credibility are the forces of gravity and magnetism. Further examples would be the way an organism's DNA shapes its growth and behaviours, or the way a principle like "survival of the fittest" is believed to have determined evolution.

Some abstractions encourage certain actions as when, say, team spirit motivates team players to try their best. The basic rules of mathematics provide another kind of abstraction with another kind of power. You cannot logically break the rules of addition, subtraction, multiplication and division and live in the real world. You can deliberately be dishonest of course, but can you really make 2+2=5?

The maths of addition and subtraction (plus countless other mathematical rules) seem to have a relationship with what we see in the physical world. If you have 4 bricks and remove 2 of them, there will be 2 left. The causal connection between removing the 2 bricks and the outcome is clear enough. Similarly, there seem to be psychological and social forces operating in the world of people, though there is more scope for ambiguity and confusion.

For example, we say a child has a built in curiosity which could be described as a drive. It incentivises the learning process. However, 'curiosity' and 'drive' and 'learning' are all abstractions, so when we make statements of this kind interpretation and definitions come into play – even if observations and surveys assume we all understand what is involved.

The bottom line here is that we recognise the reality of very many abstractions and we live our lives for the most part according to them. If you belong to a school you will believe there is an abstract reality which you will probably want to respect and for which, if you are a sportsperson, you will try hard to win games. If you are a soldier you will be willing to fight for your country which you will call something like your Motherland or Fatherland or 'Land of your Birth'. You will probably even be willing to die defending it!

If you had been an Allied soldier of WW1 unfortunate enough to be killed and buried abroad your family and friends could have drawn comfort from the sentiments of the poem "The Soldier" by Rupert Brooke, where the abstraction called 'England' is beyond any physical piece of geography.

If I should die, think only this of me:
That there's some corner of a foreign field
That is for ever England.

After Sir Bobby Charlton, a famous and much loved footballer, died in October 2023, a newspaper headline read: "With his passing, a little piece of England has died." The thought was that he had been "our bridge to loyalty and duty, to modesty and diligence...(he) came to represent much of what we thought was the best of us." So again 'England' is not an actual place, nor simply a collection of people who speak a common language and think in similar ways. It is an abstraction which captures certain values and assumptions. This abstraction is presented as having a life of its own.

A very clear-cut expression of the reality of abstractions comes from an atheist! In Comte-Sponville's interestingly entitled *The Book of Atheist Spirituality* (2009) he writes of past *moments of mystery, self-evidence, plenitude, simplicity, unity, silence, eternity, serenity, acceptance and independence.* That awareness was of *the very reality...of which I was a part* (pp188-189). He rejects the idea that this awareness is merely an internal personal experience. *How could I contain the absolute? The absolute contains me – I can reach it only by leaving myself behind* (p198).

Enduring realities are captured in places, music, etc

Our minds are constantly interpreting the world around us. We use the categories of language and the principles we have been taught or have acquired to make sense of what we see or hear. We filter out what seems irrelevant.

It is not that there is no physical or social world out there, that everything is a creation of our imaginations. That would be silly! Rather, all our knowledge and experience of the world is on a continuum in which our minds play a greater or lesser part, but never no part at all. Further, the claim here is that as humans we sense a reality that transcends what is immediately visible or tangible.

We can illustrate all this by considering the way many of us treat items from the past. We accumulate old photographs, we collect antiques, we drive classic cars, we visit old holiday haunts, etc. We sense the past – people, places, events – in what we see. You may suppose that all this reminiscence is no more than imaginative nostalgic indulgence. We can't really bring back the past, can we?

Well, why is an old song so powerful? Why not just dismiss it with a few words such as "that is all in the past, I've moved on from all that now"? After all, why should we want to accumulate clutter (physical or mental)? Well, think about this. Dealers go around collecting dated objects because they know there are committed people wanting to buy them – usually, one presumes, with a view to preserving or recreating the past in some way. Why are certain places almost sacred to us because of their associations – places where we might take a partner or grandchild to show how important they were/are to us, or perhaps the place might be so special for us that we can only go alone?

Why are certain objects imbued with unique value, such as Princess Diana's Ford Escort which sold at auction in 2022 for £650K? Here is a true story. A new wedding ring was lost in the sea during the honeymoon. Although it was possible to buy an identical ring this was not the ring which had been given in the wedding ceremony, and for the newly married couple it could never be the same.

Minds and persons

Alongside abstractions of the kind considered so far we have the reality of our mind or consciousness. Our minds are full of ideas, full of sensations and emotions – like pain or sadness or love. But if you cut open a person's brain would you see a mind? Would you see emotions? Would you see thoughts? If you were able to open up a person's head while they were dreaming would you be able to see the dream? The answer to all these is a resounding NO. You might be able to measure electrical impulses or the firing of synapses, of course, but these would just be the physical conditions or accompaniments to the thoughts and ideas. They could not be the actual thoughts. This is because, like the abstractions we have just been considering, they are invisible – yet they exist!

In short, we have thoughts and experiences which exist and are real for each person – but don't exist in a physical sense. Our minds are dependent on electrical impulses and brain parts, as we have noted, but cannot be reduced to those physical processes.

We sometimes talk about persons as if they were just bodies. 'Only 6 persons allowed in the waiting room', 'The price is £12 per person', etc. But that is not the full story. Persons have rights, they deserve protection and safeguarding, they are individuals with private thoughts, they can be creative, they can be lonely, and so on. Persons are said to deserve certain things – either rewards or punishments. Why? Because they have agency and choice. Physical, social and psychological factors may limit choice to some degree, of course. But reason provides at least some choices in life. It would not make sense to describe someone as a person if reason and choice were not part of their being.

Many people are asking whether AI (Artificial Intelligence) could ever constitute a person. Most would probably think not. But future developments might alter all that. In the same way as those who study animal behaviour might believe some higher animals (such as dolphins) deserve to be treated as persons, so it would seem unreasonable to rule out the possibility for a potential person created by AI.

Do persons change over time? Inevitably people mature, they are moulded by experience and events, their faculties might even be impaired. So after 60 or so years do we have another person? That of course is largely true of the body. Most of your body cells will be replaced every 7 years. But what about us as persons or centres of consciousness? Are we still the same person after 7 years, or 70 years?

I think most would say we were. We have the same identity: normally the same early memories (often of course modified, distorted, coloured), the same upbringing and parenting, the same early experience of relationships, and so on. There has to be some sort of continuity – otherwise how would you, *as you*, remember all the past in the intimate and personally meaningful way you do?

Over the years we will have certainly expanded our horizons in lots of ways, but we remain the same person. So change is built into our consciousness. We live with change. We live with loss and new finds. This is a very important idea to hold on to, because arguably we have the capacity to *keep on changing*. There may be a future changed dimension to our lives – a change beyond the material physical world upon which we presently depend. The spirit or consciousness arguably has qualities of endurance.

So could a mind survive the end of the brain? On the face of it, it could not, as it is dependent seemingly on the physical activity of the brain: electrical impulses, brain tissue, blood flow, etc. In fact there may be no obvious boundary between mind and body, as is suggested by developments in modern medicine and psychology. But that may only be true of life as we know it. A mind or consciousness may have a parallel independent existence in the same way as we say '7' has an existence apart from the physical world. In fact, there are plenty of cases where people claim to have out-of-body experiences eg they seem to look down on themselves during a surgical operation. Much new research seems to suggest that 'near death experiences' and other related phenomena reveal a persistence of consciousness beyond the brain and body.

The theme of this book is that there are many aspects of human experience which are suggestive of entities which endure and go beyond the physical/material. Everything changes over time. Persons are no exception. They change but they still retain their identity.

The ninth chapter develops these points further within the context of a discussion of how we face death.

Life here is incomplete: we look to future fulfilment

There is much in human experience which is suggestive of a further stage of development, or completion. A kitten would tell you it has some growing and developing to do. A half-written book or symphony invites further work. A half-built house awaits the return of the builder. These cases are pretty obvious, but so arguably are the more subtle aspects of human experience, if we think about it: learning to build depth and endurance in a loving relationship, building peace out of war, finding healing even where pain and illness remain. These all are on a trajectory. Their present state is incomplete.

In the case of a growing kitten it will not take long to see the mature animal: about a year probably. But other things seem to require a time stretching into the future and beyond. They are suggestive of something enduring or even eternal!

As we work through the chapters which follow we will apply the above considerations to the various topics to reveal aspects of our human culture and experiences which endure, or are suggestive of a future state of development.

1 TIME, timeliness and timelessness

We read and hear a lot about the management of time in our private or corporate lives, but do we stop to wonder about the sort of thing time is, or even whether it has any real existence beyond what we have been taught to think? What, if anything, is the time shown on our watches and clocks beyond an allocation of numbers to the way we divide up our lives?

There is a world of difference between the question: What is the time? and the question: What is time? The question: What is the time? Will be answered by looking at your watch or clock, and what that tells you will depend where in the world you happen to be. The range may be considerable even in one large country – like North America or Russia.

But: What is time? is a question the answer to which will not depend on where you happen to be in the world, or what your watch is telling you. So how do we begin to answer this question?

It seems to be an inescapable part of our lives. We would suppose that there has never been a period without time (except you might say before the 'Big Bang'), nor that there could be a situation in the future without time (unless you believe in an 'End of the World' scenario). For most of us such possibilities seem beyond our comprehension. It is hard to think outside the box of conventional time keeping. We are so used to having our lives regulated by the clock that we take it as a given.

Even the time scales we learn about in geology are hard enough to grasp. Perhaps our best response is simple to be awestruck by the gigantic epochs of time represented by geological formations, sometimes called 'deep time', or the millions of years which have passed since the dinosaurs walked the earth, or the millions of years light from distant stars have taken to reach us. We can only wrestle with these ideas with our finite minds. Our human lives seem like hardly anything in the vast, seemingly infinite, oceans of time.

Yet, as William Blake put it:

You may

Hold Infinity in the palm of your hand
And Eternity in an hour

(Auguries of Innocence 1863)

Similarly, we are intrigued (and baffled!) by the prospect of time-travel, as attested for example by the stream of films which have time-travel as the basis for the plot. Films such as *Back to the future, Flight of the Navigator, Bill and Ted's Excellent Adventure* or *The Adam Project.*

We have already considered an aspect of timelessness when we reflected on abstractions in the Introduction. There we noted that abstractions and mathematical truths seem timeless. Possibly there might be another universe where 2+2=5, but that would defy logic.

In the fifth chapter we will consider how certain values like truth or courage or kindness seem timeless. Could one seriously argue that they are merely fleeting and subjective? That a future civilisation may operate on the principle that it was good to lie, or to be cowardly, or to be cruel? How could communication exist if no one could be trusted to tell the truth? Of course we all see plenty of examples where truth or kindness are trampled on, but the very fact that we can sense the moral failure and feel perhaps outraged is evidence of the enduring importance of the principle.

In the eighth chapter we will consider how love seems to have a timelessness about it. Many love songs speak of love going on forever. A wedding ring – a token of enduring love – goes round and round forever. Yet paradoxically time seems to stand still at ecstatic moments.

In 'The Thornbirds' (a novel set in Australia and made into a film and television series) Meggie has fallen in love with an ambitious Catholic priest who is committed to remaining celibate. Despite this, they have one night of passion. Meggie later says that that one night can last her a lifetime. So, time both stood still and lasted a lifetime. A paradox? Yes!

But even in the physical world there are hints to suggest nothing is purely temporary. Physical things change and may seem to disappear, but their atoms and molecules are still in the universe somewhere. A person will at some point die, but what happens to the spirit or consciousness? Why think that it must simply cease to exist? In any case the ripples from that life continue forever, however subtle and invisible those future influences might be. After all, each one of us is the product of a million interactions in the lives of our forebears.

We actually have plenty of hints of what timelessness might be like – even if such examples are elusive and fleeting. Could we go on to think that time could 'flex', or could depend on the observer or participant? In the Special Theory of Relativity, Einstein determined that time is relative—in other words, the rate at which time passes depends on your frame of reference. This sounds counter-intuitive. How could it be that when scientists synchronized two highly accurate atomic clocks and then flew one around the Earth aboard an aeroplane, afterwards the airborne clock was a fraction of a second behind the one that remained on the ground? Or that time moves differently for someone below sea level compared with someone situated on a high peak? Or that if you could travel at the speed of light you would not experience a sense of time? Or that it might even be possible (though admittedly unlikely) to travel back and forth in time, as in science fiction? Or that literally no time at all is needed for atomic particles which are entangled to affect each other over huge distances?

Less baffling is the way culture and language affect perception of time, thus making it appear to flex. It is a common experience that different cultural groups seem to have varying ways of measuring time and determining when events occur. For some, timing events by the clock will be more important than letting them run their course. Punctuality may be more, or less, critical.

There has been much academic discussion in linguistics about the way particular languages dispose native speakers to think of time in particular ways. Some languages, such as Japanese, are claimed to have no barrier between the future and the present tense, whereas others, including English, are said to make a clear distinction between these tenses. The implication is that these differences may affect the way present time and future time are perceived and understood.

The fact that we for the most part try to make the best use of time suggests we respect time – even the way it slips through our fingers and has elusive qualities. 'Tempus fugit' (time flies) is a phrase you sometimes see on a clock face.

We seek to find ways to get the most out of time. We attend courses, or read books, on time management. We tend to chide ourselves if we feel we are wasting time on something. Most of us try to use time in ordinary life thoughtfully and creatively. If we have spare time we tend to use it to develop a hobby or learn something new or socialise. If we are sufficiently dedicated to the hobby we ensure that we make time for it.

Time is so much more than minutes and hours. A key point must be that if a person can feel themselves in control of time (within the constraints we all know about and face) they are on the road to a deeper appreciation of what time means and what timelessness might be like. Time is the starting point to thinking about what might endure or go beyond conventional time-keeping.

Think of time as like a river. It flows. 'Time like an everflowing stream' is a phrase from Psalm 90 in the Hebrew Bible. But while it flows with a certain inevitability, it can to an extent be controlled (as, say, when people or beavers alter river flows) and it can certainly be used in advantageous ways when its water is dependable (as when water is stored in a dam and used for irrigation).

The rate of turbulence in the water depends on the width of the stream, obstructions and the gradient of the river. The deep parts of the river may seem still, though there is still a flow. There are eddies and counter-currents. Ultimately the river will flow into the sea and become part of the seemingly eternal ebb and flow of currents and waves.

So think of time as flexing – just as water in a stream. Sometimes time seems to stand still. This could be a supremely joyous thing as in an ecstatic experience, mentioned above. Or it could be very negative, as waiting for hours at an airport. 'Time drags' we then say. To continue the metaphor of the river or stream, we might think of the occasions when the river temporarily freezes over.

In all these sorts of situations the trick is to treasure the time, to nurture it, to think about how to use it creatively. For example in difficult situations – such as in a health crisis – one might say 'One day at a time' and focus on managing the situation step by step, minute by minute even. Equally, one might focus on a week or month ahead, looking to future happiness as a target to get through a present crisis.

To an extent time commands us, but it is also ours to command. If we manage our time effectively (we have already noted that there are plenty of books and courses on how to do this) we seem to be able to get more done: to seemingly make time. We have all heard the saying: 'If you want something done, give it to a busy person.'

But though we don't usually choose to 'mark time' or waste time, use of time for leisure – to relax, to chat, to meditate – has its place, and with serious important tasks we would be well advised to 'take our time'.

The author of Ecclesiastes in the Hebrew Bible reminds us 'To everything there is a season, and a time to every purpose under the heaven.'

The Greek God Chronos used some of his time for destructive disgusting purposes (eg eating his own children). His life came to symbolise the way time could be used perniciously and fail to bring comfort or satisfaction. We destroy others and ourselves. A less horrifying – indeed very hilarious – way of getting that same message across is in the film Clockwise (1986) where John Cleese plays a time-obsessed headteacher whose best laid plans fall apart.

Instead of being governed, driven even, by the clock, we could consider the model of the Greek god Kairos – the god of timely grasping of opportunity. A particular moment in time may be the ideal moment for fulfilling a certain quest or need.

Four year olds are not at the right age to learn trigonometry, but they are at the ideal age for acquiring language. Some people find they are most productive in the morning or evening. And so it goes on.

But in order to judge the right time to do something you have to see what has come before and what the future may hold. Chronos obsesses with the present – it is all important and lives are governed by timelines and schedules. Kairos takes the longer view and sees everything in its wider context. Kairos looks to the future.

This point can easily be illustrated by comparing a digital watch with a traditional analogue watch. A digital watch only gives you the time now, but a traditional analogue watch, with its clock face, contextualises the present moment. You can easily see how much time you have spent on a given activity and how much time is left.

The analogue watch encourages us to think of time organically or holistically. That is perhaps a more telling point than it may seem at first sight. Our lives flow. Each moment has emerged from what has gone before, and the present moment passes on something to the next. To an extent there is a logical sequence to each life: birth, growing up, early adulthood, late adulthood, old age, death.

Some people would want to say that time has a spiritual dimension, by which they might mean that time gives rise to deep reflective questions. Are we grateful for the time we have? Or do we fear the passage of time? Are there timeless qualities we seek to discover or reveal, or do we live only for the moment? Do we go about our day with a light or heavy heart?

Most questions in life are time related. A basic question might be how to choose to spend time to earn one's living, and how much time to spend in training or preparation. Time (to an extent) is money. A related question is determining the right time to move on professionally and how best to do so. A further question might be what work-life balance is appropriate and how much time to allocate to various leisure pursuits. For some a question might be how much time to give to bringing up children.

Other dimensions might be the time we spend on ourselves relative to the time we spend helping others, or how we define quality time.

However, it would be a mistake to believe there is always only one right answer. Just as the water in the river can seemingly 'choose' to flow in a quiet deep place or over some rapids, so there may not be one right thing to do (though choices are inevitable, as is the flow of the river). Life is not that simple, and we shouldn't beat ourselves up over the poor choices we may have made. In fact, it is far better to think of the way past choices have enhanced our awareness — how we can learn from past experiences. In any case, for good or ill each one of us is where we are and must go forward with our lives as best we may.

So how can time flex for you? How can you go with the inevitable flow, while retaining control? How can you contemplate the passage of time in a creative, life enhancing way? How can you slay the Chronos god who gobbles up time (and gobbles up life itself) and embrace the Kairos god who chooses the right time for everything? What can you learn about savouring, treasuring timeless places, objects and memories?

Our memories are held in a time-related way. This becomes very apparent in some forms of dementia where early memories are vivid while recent ones fade. And while some of the entities we regard as enduring, do so through time, others seem to defy any notion of time – as in the case of an abstraction like 7.

But all the above reflections on time – how to use it wisely and creatively – inevitably point to a certain conclusion: *that we aspire to something beyond time*. As a person ages they may sense that there will be unfinished business – projects awaiting further development. This may be especially so if there has been some impairment in later life which has restricted what activities are possible.

You would be very fortunate if you could say in the last days of your life 'I've done everything I wanted to, and am content to go.' Most people are interested in staying alive as long as possible providing they have a reasonable quality of life. You only have to read a few popular magazines to realise that there is a lively interest in healthy eating, suitable exercise, latest medical advances, etc. Most people want more time! However, despite every best effort each life will come to an end.

So could we aspire to live without time – or at least in a way that seeks out what is timeless? Those who practise mindfulness – the idea to focus attention on the present moment, to appreciate the detail or charm along each step we take – have a special insight into the way time may morph into timelessness. As the philosopher Wittgenstein put it 100 years ago:

> If by eternity is understood not endless temporal duration, but timelessness, then he lives eternally who lives in the present.

In the half million waking hours the average person might expect in a lifetime there will have been enough experiences which touch on timeless things to suggest there is something beyond time. In other words we have time to sense that time could be up for time itself! The clock will not have the last word.

2 MUSIC has timeless aspects

We take music as our main exemplar of an aesthetic dimension of human experience.

Many people have found that music has the ability to move hearts and minds. Political leaders have used music to boost morale and loyalty. Hence we have all encountered army bands and patriotic or nationalist songs. Religions use music to stir or express the emotions, and so it goes on.

So apart from the ability to move hearts and minds, what else?

Music has aesthetic qualities. It does more than move hearts. Like any aesthetic form – art, sculpture, architecture, dance, drama, etc – it touches on a dimension of life which seems timeless. Of course, what counts as beautiful music (or art, etc) will vary from culture to culture and even person to person to some extent, but is *all* beauty in the eye of the beholder, or in the case of music is beautiful music in the ear of the listener? Is it that subjective?

No, that surely can't be right. You can listen to a new piece of music and not like it at all. But after listening to it several times you might come to realise that you have missed something. The music has a quality which is beyond your personal taste.

It is probably going to be quite controversial defining what those qualities of excellence are (and they will vary depending on the type of music – jazz, classical, easy listening, and so on). But the fact that musicians attempt such definitions, and budding musicians will seek to follow the lead of established musicians, suggests that the quest for definition is not in vain. What would be the point of pursuing quality or beauty in music unless there were the belief that the goal was achievable?

In other fields of aesthetics we look to supposed experts to judge standards. The experts may disagree, but they will be using criteria and interpreting how far they have been met. Take the TV programme *Strictly Come Dancing*. There you will hear the judges applying their criteria for quality in dancing. They will comment on aspects like: following the rhythm and tempo, finesse of movement, expressing character and personality, harmonising as a couple, originality, degree of difficulty, wise choice of dance/music, etc.

Sometimes the judges will dispute among themselves, but what they dispute about is not random. Thus, although subjectivity has a place so do the criteria and standards to which the judges refer.

Some people will argue that big business has a role in determining standards and tastes in music, as in other areas of artistic creation. Clearly, there is commercial interest in selling new styles and fashions in music as in anything else. But to suppose that commercial interest is the *sole* arbiter of quality or standards is facile (and actually demeaning of creative people).

Does a tune exist even if no one is playing it, or even thinking about it? Would it still be a beautiful piece of music even if there were no people left in the world to listen to it?

If you are inclined to answer YES to these questions you are not needing to be convinced that there are timeless qualities to music. The qualities go beyond what is simply a matter of opinion or feeling.

You would probably want to say that all music has common roots, despite cultural variation. Equally, you would probably think that there are at least some cross-cultural standards by which music, or any artistic creation or performance, is judged, and that such standards have enduring features.

But there lots of other possible ways in which music touches on timeless qualities. In music we inevitably must interpret sounds. We receive vibrations through the air and our minds convert these vibrations into music – providing they match what we feel are the standards applied to judging what counts as music. Even if you think all judgements in music are purely subjective, it is still true that we have to interpret the vibrations which enter our

13

ears. The process will hint at something fundamental and timeless – that music exists and is to be distinguished from noise. Some would want to say that the ability to appreciate or discern music could be a mark of what it is to be a person.

There are various further reasons for thinking that music may give us access to an invisible realm which may have permanency.

Human emotion through music

Music certainly moves us beyond what might be called the bare necessities or basics of life.

A performance of great music can temporarily uplift us and remove us from anxieties. Equally it can be sombre and make us gloomy and sad. Some seem to find that they are transported into another dimension or state. At an extreme they may claim a tranquil state of ecstasy. They may feel at one with humankind or the world, in a realm of peace.

This may be particularly true of those who compose or play music. Haydn when completing *The Creation* in 1801 reportedly claimed to be feeling more devout. Stravinsky would have agreed that this could be so. In his lectures delivered at Harvard in 1939–40 he argued that the meaning of music and its main aim was to promote

a communion, a union of man
with his fellow man and with the Supreme Being.

These states of feeling or emotion share a kind of timelessness. They share in an ongoing flood of such experiences which have no beginning or end.

While on the one hand music can arouse, invigorate or inspire, it can also express pain: fear, unrequited love, bereavement, for example.

The composer Arnold Schoenberg, having witnessed the chaos and horror of two world wars and feeling deeply moved, wrote a profound cantata *A survivor from Warsaw*. This came to be seen as one of the greatest cultural memorials to the Holocaust. It certainly went far beyond a form of entertainment. It brought alive the past in a striking way which gave it lasting quality of remembrance.

Another piece of music which is a memorial to the horrors of war is Benjamin Britten's War Requiem, performed for the first time in the new Coventry Cathedral in 1962. The ruin of the old medieval cathedral stands on the same site, equally a public statement of outrage against war, conflict and violence. In similar ways classical symphonies, as any music with enduring quality, become rather like vast archives of public memory.

Such feelings of anguish, emptiness, and hopelessness seem like the very opposite of peace or ecstasy. But maybe there is a relationship. We can only experience true ecstasy if we can live also with the sadness. That is perhaps a perennial truth, expressed in musical variety.

Thus music may represent the reality of life with its ups and downs, its sadnesses and its joys. Maybe some music can help us reconcile the different elements in our lives. This is not so much transporting us to another realm as helping us to live better in the world as we find it. But it expresses an enduring truth.

The poet Christina Rossetti (1830-1894) used the metaphor of musical harmony to capture this idea.

Tune me, O Lord, into one harmony
With Thee, one full responsive vibrant chord;
Unto Thy praise all love and melody,
Tune me, O Lord.

Thus need I flee nor death, nor fire, nor sword:
A little while these be, then cease to be,
And sent by Thee not these should be abhorred.

Many stories told through music move from darkness to light, and the light seems all the brighter for having passed through the dark.

Within a piece of music there will often be parts which are in a minor or sad key which then 'come right', so to speak, when the major or happy key is restored.

So music has the potential to take us to what some may call a spiritual place. Some might see this as a state of ecstacy. Some might find this to be a realm where contradictions can be reconciled and harmonised.

Music an appetiser for something further

Arguably for many of us music functions as a sort of appetiser to something we never quite attain. There are blemishes and uncertainties in it which could be deliberate or inadvertent. There seems to be the aspiration to something beyond – at present we are dissatisfied. That speaks of the way we are made. We have a built in predisposition to seek for something beyond ourselves. If this is a forlorn hope in our present lives, it suggests we may be destined for something better. So music points beyond itself to a realm where time will not be as we know it at present – if it exists at all.

Universals in music

Let's further develop the idea of musical universals. Although there are all kinds of different music and significant cultural variants, as we have noted, what might be the musical universals which underpin *all* music? Part of the case for this is that musical harmonies are derived from mathematical rules which are independent of human reasoning.

It may of course be the case that what is seen as universal and timeless is really just a reflection of the Western tonal system. Some are not convinced that the acoustic principles of Western convention are really mathematically demonstrated, rather than man-made. But let's stick with it for a moment.

To take a simple example in the Western musical tradition, the note 'c' is still c whether it is sung high by a soprano voice or low by a bass voice. The c's are separated by one or more octaves, and each note has a frequency which has a mathematical relationship to all the other c notes (the frequency doubles for each octave). Thus, given that the note c sounds fine to our ears when sung by both a soprano and a bass voice, we could say the roots of music may be derived from something about the natural world. In other words our ears reveal to us a universal enduring truth about music.

On the other hand, there are certain combinations of notes which sound dark or unsettling. The notes c and f sharp together give such an uncomfortable sound. The dark sound can be anywhere on the scale with the right space between the notes. Technically this is a Tritone, but in popular musical culture it has been known as The Devil's Interval. Usually it has been shunned, but it was used to good effect in Benjamin Britten's War Requiem (mentioned above) to express the fear of war, and it can be heard in modern times in some heavy metal music.

So in short there could be universal truths embedded in the rich symphonies of music – truths which are not temporary or passing. Even if individual pieces of music were to cease to be heard, the truths embedded in music would endure.

Let's take this a stage further. Arguably, music like any art form is concerned with universals in an *extended* sense. Music may tell a certain story, or reflect the aesthetic of a particular composer, but it goes beyond that. It may convey an abstract quality: pain, joy, peace of mind, fear, courage, etc.

In the world of art, a picture may be of a mother and child, but to be true art some would say it must speak of something like maternal tenderness.

This is paralleled in music by Wagner's famous remark:

> *What Music expresses is eternal, infinite, and ideal; she expresses not the passion, love, desire, of this or that individual in this or that condition, but Passion, Love, Desire itself...*

Thus, music may provide a window on the human condition – something like: 'we are emotional beings with a range of fears, hopes and fantasies'. These could be said to be enduring truths or abstractions about humankind providing insight into the intrinsic power of the emotions which comprise human life.

Great works of art, whether paintings or sculpture, or music may be said to have their standing precisely because they go beyond the particular to convey universal truths about what it means to be human. A portrait gallery for example might not be simply telling us what particular individuals looked like. It could be stating that we are all different individuals, we have a moral entitlement to be respected, we have an aspiration to be remembered by posterity, and so on.

3 RITUAL – a window on transcendence

So much of our lives consists of rituals of various kinds. The rituals that are significant for our discussion are not the mechanical actions which involve daily living, such as getting washed, dressing, eating, and so on, but the rituals which are recognised as having some further meaning and significance. Of course, many of the mechanical rituals can, in certain circumstances, also have this further purpose. Thus washing can be purely mechanical, but it can also serve a religious purpose, as for faithful Muslims, who before praying 5 times a day must purify themselves for meeting with Allah by washing their faces, hands, arms and feet.

These further purposes can be extremely varied. At a macro level many have argued they serve the purpose of binding members of a group or society together in shared purposes and meanings. Ritual thus helps ensure the survival of the collective. Others have highlighted a control element: an initiation rite imposes a set of expectations on the newly initiated, for example.

At the micro level of everyday life rituals can achieve all sorts of things: for example, convey friendship, as in a handshake, or a legal commitment, as when a person signs to buy or sell property.

Most rituals embody or demonstrate something of what the purpose is. Thus at a university graduation ceremony those graduating will wear academic robes as an indication of changing status. At a wedding a ring is given, or more commonly these days rings are exchanged, to signify lifelong commitment and fidelity.

Let's take a wedding as a case study. Does this wedding ritual create the marriage itself? Could it perhaps be a trick we play on ourselves, or is played on us by others, to make something seem important? Is the wedding perhaps just a game we choose to participate in, making it a special occasion to impress our friends or to satisfy convention or for legal reasons? Is the wedding ritual simply words and gestures – something ephemeral? Is it perhaps really nothing?

Perhaps the ritual is comparable to the story of the Emperor who, along with his subjects, had been persuaded that only stupid people could fail to see that he was wearing the most wonderful clothes – when the reality was he was not wearing anything at all. Perhaps we should be like the young lad who was not taken in by the hype and could call out the truth: the Emperor was wearing nothing at all. Only in this case it is not so much about non-existent clothes (though some wedding outfits reveal quite a lot!) as the imaginary event of the wedding itself – if that is what we believe.

However, this is not the way we typically use the idea of a wedding in ordinary life. Most of us think of it as a 'something', though undoubtedly this view is not universal. It is NOT ephemeral most people will say. The wedding ceremony may not necessarily be religious, or even thought of as 'spiritual', but few would say it was 'nothing'. To simply point to its implications (eg financial commitments, or the right of children to inherit a title), or to say that it is likely to impact one's intentions, emotions, feelings, and beliefs, is to sidestep the issue. A married person may flout all the conventions and expectations of a marriage (neglect children, reject inherited titles, take other partners, etc), but the marriage will still be held to exist (unless deemed to be void or voidable for legal reasons).

In short, the marriage is an abstraction which nevertheless is real and exists. It doesn't exist in a way that can be measured or observed, though of course we can see evidence suggestive of its existence in various ways. And it rests within the framework of a society – which is also an abstraction!

There are many people who really believe marriage is for life. For them it is an abstraction which endures and cannot be destroyed.

Some might say a particular marriage was "made in heaven" and further believe it continues in an afterlife. They might say that they do not feel free to remarry after a divorce or even after the death of the spouse.

None of the above proves anything of course, but it is highly suggestive of how an institution like marriage may seem to have enduring qualities.

A particular marriage involves one level of abstraction. But it is also part of marriage as a *general* feature within human institutional life, as previously noted. A particular marriage gains credibility because it is part of something bigger. A particular marriage may last a certain number of years – perhaps even forever as some believe. But the *concept* of marriage is at a higher level. It definitely seems to have a timeless quality.

So as we review the nature and meaning of marriage we find ourselves stepping beyond what is tangible.

Rituals can take us outside the material physical world in further ways. This is most obviously the case for religious believers who may speak of the rituals of sacraments. A sacrament would be defined by some as an outward visible sign of an inward spiritual grace (gift of God working within a person). The ritual seems to make something happen. In the Communion service some believers are persuaded that in the act of Consecration the bread and wine become the body and blood of Jesus. In a Baptism (often called a Christening) the child or adult becomes a member of the church – not any particular church, most would say, but of the mystical spiritual church often described as Christ's body.

Ritual points us beyond the immediate and what is tangible. It is an acknowledgement that there is something that we cannot properly articulate – the gestures and words are pointers to a believed reality that defies description or analysis. We capture this as best we can, but it is elusive.

We are meaning makers. That seems a fundamental truth which carries us forward as human beings, and part of that meaning is the sense of what lies beyond what appears on the surface. Some of the meaning may only be something that defies intellectual understanding. In the same way as cultural artefacts like art, story, dance, music, etc seek to present an idea which resists precise definition, so ritual orients us to seek that unseen world. Rituals speak of mystery and lead us to step into it.

If ritual is an intrinsic part of what it is to be human, and there is plenty of archaeological and current evidence for believing this, then we have a clue to what we should be seeking to find through the experience of ritual: lasting reality.

4 Each PLACE holds a story

You don't have to be mystical or religious to find that certain places, or objects, seem to have a special pull or significance for us. We may claim an attachment to such places. We may feel there is something a particular place has to impart to us. Others may experience a feeling of surrendering to a place.

Sometimes this can be a collective or community thing – as with places of pilgrimage to sacred sites. Similarly, great rocks (mountains, particular peaks), lakes and springs, confluences of water and sky and burial sites have been communal power places.

Most countries will have their special awesome places. For example, in the USA Sedona, in Italy St Peter's Basilica, in Egypt the Great Pyramid, in England Stonehenge, in Greece Delphi.

There is much interest these days in the way buildings or open areas can better provide foundations for constructing group identity or in offering restorative space. City planners factor in such considerations.

A church or monument builds a sense of community and continuity with those who have gone before. A war memorial can be a source of national pride. A communal memorial can bring shared solidarity in the face of terrorism (as with the Memorial in Lockerbie Scotland to those who lost their lives when an airliner was brought down by a terrorist bomb).

Other places may be very personal or individual. Typically, there will be happy associations: perhaps a childhood association, a memorable holiday destination or a place where you first met your partner. On the other hand a particular place may seem to speak to you of an unpleasant past event and you may feel uncomfortable. People may speak of a bad feeling about a place. In extreme cases they may speak of an evil presence.

It would be easy to dismiss these feelings for places as entirely subjective, perhaps as inventions of an over active imagination. No doubt there can be some validity in this argument. But perfectly rational cool-headed people also claim these experiences. For example, it is very common to feel that the grave of a loved one is special in some way – even though it is obvious that there is no living being there. For some families it might be vital that a body is buried in a particular grave space – even though from a rational point of view it can't make any difference to the deceased person.

But a graveyard is more than a place of rest for a particular person. Visiting a graveyard deepens the sense of community, for community consists of relationships with people from the past, as well as from the present and the future. All graveyards have a story to tell about timelessness.

In any case, a place (like anything in the world) is always more than simply a physical thing. It inevitably has to be contextualised and interpreted, taking account of particular interests like architecture, history, or past personal experiences. Part of a place is what we imagine it could be. Sure, it is part of the landscape or a human construction but it is also simultaneously in people's minds, in human culture, in human practices.

While we seem to receive something such as comfort or encouragement or rehabilitation from special places, we also leave something of ourselves there. At first this might seem far-fetched, but a little thought confirms its truth. Sites or buildings or treasured artefacts have achieved their status because of the association with those who have gone before us. It is partly because others have found something special and have affirmed this by their presence that *we* now are attracted to a place or object and find it significant.

A sacred object or place will have acquired status through the practice or belief of devotees over a period of time. The fact that the story of its origins might be implausible is not necessarily detracting from its significance. (Glastonbury in England would be an excellent example. That the legend that Jesus came with Joseph of Arimathea to visit Glastonbury is hardly credible does not matter too much.)

In similar ways, by our association with a place or object we add *our* layer of endorsement on top of all the other "signatures" of those who have been there before. We become part of a tourist or pilgrimage trail which will impact others.

Some would say that there is a further way in which we might leave part of ourselves in a place. Perhaps places can hold trace memories of visitors or residents and the actions associated with them. There are many who believe they can retrieve something of earlier traces when they visit a place (although they may struggle to offer a scientific explanation). By the same token they might believe they leave their own trace when they visit. This might go some way in explaining why a house, for example, might feel like a good, or bad, place to be, a point we will return to in the tenth chapter.

The above considerations can contribute in so many ways to improving human well-being: tourism, urban regeneration, mental health, for example. But unless folk are encouraged to focus attention in creative imaginative ways on the places they visit much potential is lost. *Mindfulness* may capture what is needed.

This might be the way it could work for an individual:

> Focus attention on what seems special about a place – any place where you happen to be. Ask yourself who might have been there before, or how it came to be there or achieve importance. For example, some people are wowed

by an ancient cathedral, not just for its spiritual significance but by the passion and skill that the builders may have had. Let the place "speak" to you. Be curious about how it could inspire or help you, or what experience or memory you could take from it. Try to be open and non-judgemental. Perhaps take away a photograph or recording.

Think what you can do to enhance the experience of the place for *others* – such as a message in a visitor's book, a text-message or picture to email out, a special memory to share in conversation with a friend. Some people would say they can leave a memory trace embedded. In these ways you potentially share something of yourself with the place.

Anyone who will give a place or object their full mindful attention may be surprised how enriching the experience could be for them personally *and* for others.

5 Our sense of RIGHT and WRONG

Many people will say something like:

"What is right or wrong is merely a matter of opinion. It all depends on how a person is brought up and the culture of where they live. Look at attitudes to owning land, for example. Some cultures, such as that of First Nation Americans, believe that all land is communal – no one person or family can own any of it. Not so generally in most other cultures, where private land ownership is considered a right.

Or look at attitudes to slavery. A majority of people used to think it was fine to own slaves and make money from their labour. Not so today. And so we could go on."

While there is certainly some truth in the above, and it is arguably very important to consider the way moral codes are shaped by society and circumstance, it is only a part of the story.

It cannot just be a matter of opinion, for example, as to whether it is right to steal. There might be particular circumstances which would justify stealing – say where the only way to feed your family is by stealing food. But there is a clear presumption that normally stealing is wrong. The same would be true of telling lies, and a host of other actions which would be universally condemned.

Where do our notions of Forgiveness or Punishment fit in, unless we have a notion of right and wrong? How could you forgive someone for something which is only wrong according to one opinion? Equally, where is the justice in punishing someone for an action which only you think is wrong?

But at a very fundamental level we would think that there must be some basis for reaching moral judgements, otherwise 'right' and 'wrong' are simply forms of influence and control. This idea is explored further below.

Apparent sharp differences in what is regarded as right and wrong may be less stark when closely analysed. The differences may be derived from false premises. For example, once fuller psychological and biological understanding of gay sex emerged many of those who condemned gay sex changed their position.

These days we are waking up to the true nature of past actions in history. If we think again of slavery, we should remember that many white people used to think that black people were sub-human, that they couldn't think or feel like a proper human being would. To use black people to labour in sugar or cotton plantations would be akin to using horses or oxen to pull ploughs or carry burdens or pull heavy loads. Black slaves could be sold and traded as if they were animals.

But once the myth of racial inferiority was exposed, the whole slavery edifice came tumbling down. For it goes against the principle of human rights. Black people really are proper people!

Regardless of what other people may think of our actions, most of us will feel guilt and shame from time to time. These seem like universal categories of human experience. Maybe you might want to say that this is because of the way you have been brought up to think and feel, and that our feelings have become habituated: there is nothing *really* bad or shameful about the action. Could this be the total explanation? No! Many people will feel guilt or shame even when they are told that their upbringing is responsible. Sometimes a person falsely blames themselves for something that went wrong and feels guilt. Perhaps on occasion such guilt *can* be removed by showing the person they were not responsible (this is often a move that a counsellor might make). But guilt and shame will still have a place in other parts of their human experience.

There are universal categories of immoral actions which are captured in concepts like greed, selfishness, spitefulness, etc, and equally categories of action which enshrine positives like faithfulness, fairness, respect for others, etc. Pride can be a desirable quality as when we speak of taking pride in your work, or it can have negative connotations as when we speak of narcissistic or hubristic pride.

What are our grounds for making these ethical or moral judgements? Well, various explanations have been offered. Perhaps we just have an intuition as to what is fundamentally right or good. Some might call that a conscience. Perhaps we believe that 'God' or some universal power determines what is right or good and our religion alerts us to this. Perhaps we simply reason our way to an ethical understanding: we have a sense of fairness and justice guided by the 'golden rule' that we should only do to others what we would be prepared for them to do to us.

For the purposes of this discussion, it doesn't really matter what the origin of our moral code is. The point is that there are principles which we believe are not arbitrary. For us, they exist in some way – even if we might be mistaken. But even being mistaken about something assumes that there is some principle which would *not* be mistaken – something which would be valid. We wouldn't argue about differences in moral values unless we thought there was something at stake.

The key point is that if someone asserts that what is right or wrong is simply a matter of convention or opinion in the same way as a preference for carrots over parsnips, or the colour green over yellow, is simply a matter of taste, we must surely say that that is not good enough. That it simply does not do justice to the way we as humans think and act.

So our ethical principles are brilliant pointers to enduring realities. They exist beyond any particular view or culture.

6 The call of NATURE

As we explore the concept of nature we realise that it is an abstraction derived from a multitude of images and experiences. We can select an image for nature but it will inevitably be just a fragment of what we sense nature to be about. So long as there has been life on earth, nature has existed, and the abstraction may be said to have existed before that. And so it will continue. Thus nature in all its richness and diversity speaks of something enduring and timeless, and as we as humans share in nature so we share in that timelessness.

If we define nature in simple terms as the life of living things — flora and fauna — and then think of where we usually expect to find this nature it would probably be in the countryside, perhaps walking in a wood or examining at close quarters a rabbit warren or the droppings of a deer. There are gradations of this simple picture. For example, an open green space in a city connects us only to a limited extent with nature, whereas deep in a Siberian forest we would probably feel closer. In fact, we are unlikely to find much 'pure' or pristine nature. This is because human intervention will almost certainly have brought about at least subtle changes. A forest, for example, may be 'managed', animal life will reflect what has gone on in the past by way of hunting and what is going on now in the surrounding areas, plant life will have been affected by chemicals (as for example in the case of acid rain), and so on.

Nevertheless, wherever a place of nature is on the scale of human intervention, we can be wowed, inspired, consoled, refreshed by being in that space.

> *To the attentive eye, each moment of the year has its own beauty, and in the same field, it beholds, every hour, a picture which was never seen before, and which shall never be seen again. The heavens change every moment, and reflect their glory or gloom on the plains beneath.*
>
> (Ralph Waldo Emerson 1803-1882)

As such, we can be lifted into another realm where time can stand still, the world is benign, and we see and feel beyond the material.

And the call of nature is strong. Garden Centres capitalise on this. House plants find a ready sale in cities. The removal of a tree can spark major protest. Parks are jealously protected. Greenbelt might be being lost – but under protest. National parks are faithfully maintained. And so it goes on. We value green space for many reasons, no doubt, but its intrinsic connection with nature is surely high priority. Nature truly does wow and inspire, etc, taking us to new heights.

But remember that we are inevitably observing to a greater or lesser extent the human intervention that has taken, or is taking, place. And therein lies a further vital truth. Whatever nature means to us, it would be misleading to think of it as providing some sort of distraction from everyday life. It *is* everyday life. We are all part of nature, and our wellbeing is part and parcel of the wellbeing of nature. We exist within a complex ecosystem which we could think of as an extension of our own body.

> *Nature, in its ministry to man, is not only the material, but is also the process and the result. All the parts incessantly work into each other's hands for the profit of man. The wind sows the seed; the sun evaporates the sea; the wind blows the vapour to the field; the ice, on the other side of the planet, condenses rain on this; the rain feeds the plant; the plant feeds the animal; and thus the endless circulations of the divine charity nourish man.*
>
> Ralph Waldo Emerson

Thus all the things we might choose to say about nature we are also indirectly saying about ourselves. So what might we say we learn about ourselves? That there is constant change and evolution in all sorts of ways, not least through the seasons. That we have seasons in our lives. That the flora and fauna have adapted to survive and thrive in those seasonal changes, as we try to. That life and death are part of an ongoing story of Life with a capital L (ie Life, rather than one particular life). That there is much that is fragile and mysterious.

Let's consider these aspects, and their application to human beings, under the following headings.

Change and evolution

The evolution of different species is astonishing. Very few creatures are like crocodiles which have remained virtually unchanged for over 200 million years. The way domestic dogs in all their varieties have been bred (from wolves supposedly) is amazing (and testimony again to human interaction with nature). There are many, many comparable examples.

As noted in the Introduction, as persons we are constantly changing, though somehow we hold our identities with particular histories, etc. We adapt to changing circumstances (probably more rapidly than in the animal or plant kingdom). We change through a lifetime of perhaps 90 years to some extent in sync with nature, and maybe there is a further story of change beyond that.

The changing seasons

We speak of the seasons of life, of course not always corresponding with the climatic seasons. But the idea that there are particular periods of life – childhood, working life, retirement, etc – is helpful for reflecting on what might be most fruitful for that period. The climatic seasons of winter and summer etc are really appreciated by many folk, even if they will prefer one season over another. They value the changes and variety. So we can learn to value the seasons of our lives.

There is a predictability to the seasons, even if winters tend to be less severe than years ago and summers can be hotter and wetter. The idea of the cycle of the seasons is important. However gloomy a winter may be, spring is never far away. But no sooner spring and summer than autumn and winter!

The seasons of life mirror to some extent the climatic seasons. We may borrow the climatic vocabulary. The autumn of life to suggest ageing. Spring to suggest starting out in life. Winter to be associated with a time of sadness – the winter of discontent.

However, there is a positive story to be told about each season. For example, the colour of the trees and the falling leaves in Autumn. The coziness of gathering around a log fire at Christmas time and the beauty of the snow on the hills. And let's resist the idea that winter is a time of death. Yes, some shrubs will die, but most vegetation survives – possibly in dormant fashion. Some animals are well adapted to winter conditions, while others may hibernate. In fact, winter is a vital time for most flora and fauna of a particular place.

So the seasons of our lives should not hold fear. Like the climatic seasons, they are all about continuity through change. Life with a capital L. It would not only be futile to resist the inevitability of the pattern of life processes. It would actually be damaging, as we would thereby miss out on the opportunities of each part. But good luck to those who think they can achieve endless life by the use of a technology like Cryonics!

Life and death in nature

Whatever we might say about the continuity of Life with a capital L, the reality for individual plants and animals is that they will die. DNA determines likely lifespans and to some extent inclinations, instincts and capabilities. That is part of the natural order. Animals seem to accept their deaths once their decline has set in – even if they will put up a fight to survive while they are able. So there is a message there of acceptance of the inevitability of physical death.

There is a remarkably relevant slogan used by the Marie Curie charity in promoting its work with end-of-life patients, 'Death is not the opposite of life; it is part of life'. This insight into the way death is a natural part of life speaks volumes.

All living things will seek to propagate their own kind – to pass on life to the next generation. That is a vote for life. Life is a positive! As humans we put a humanistic spin on that. On the whole, we would say life is good (otherwise why would we be sad when a young person dies without experiencing much of life's pleasures?).

But we take it a stage further. Most of us yearn for something eternal. As noted previously, the Hebrew Bible puts it in Ecclesiastes 3:11: God has 'set eternity in the human heart'.

Arguably this is part of what nature has given us and so we assume it serves some purpose. This is not so much wishful thinking, as some people suggest, as a sense of logical progression. We have what seems to be a sort of instinct or natural intuitive insight. So again we repeat a recurring theme from earlier chapters: we look for completion, we sense there is some further stage to whatever we try to do or achieve in this life, we have a sense of bringing things to fruition.

So, if like all living things our physical body dies, we hope for some sort of bearing of fruit, some kind of completion beyond our 70–90 odd years here. We experience change within ourselves throughout our lives, so the idea of change through death and beyond does not seem too farfetched.

Fragility and Mystery

Rachel Carson's *Silent Spring* (1962) is usually credited with alerting the world to the fragility of nature. The Spring she imagined was silent because there were no birds to sing, and there were no birds because of the poisonous effects of DDT and allied products.

Since then all sorts of threats to nature have been identified, mostly due to human activity. However, thanks to numerous conservation efforts some restorations have been occurring. For example, the Peregrine Falcon, facing extinction in 1967, is now breeding again – sometimes in surprising urban places. Many would see this as showing the potential for regeneration and the way humans can co-exist with wild nature. The regeneration of river systems is another example of recovery.

So while nature is fragile and very vulnerable, it may recover with help. As such, we see illustrations of the principle of continuity – if we try hard enough to make this happen. Life can go on, but maybe not quite in the same old way.

Climate change may pose a real problem. Adapting to the rapid changes may be impossible for some plants, animals and people. We could say that the processes of nature which have been running for millennia have a slow rhythm and life of their own. We disrupt that time-honoured rhythm at our peril.

All nature is at heart a mystery. At school you probably learned NOT to probe the mystery. You were told, for example, to accept that plants manufacture starch by photosynthesis, pollination occurs thanks to insects taking pollen from stamen to stigma. Don't ask any further questions! Just label the diagram correctly and you will get a tick and a mark! This failure to celebrate mystery – to instead present understanding of the world as if it were information in a convenient box – impoverishes human understanding and thwarts human flourishing. Why? Because mystery and uncertainty are at the heart of our world.

Thus, for example, animal migration has fascinated humans for centuries. Scientists have shed light on some of the enduring mysteries about how species navigate and what drives them to leave a habitat, but there will always be further questions. The Monarch butterfly migrates 3000 miles, in multi-generations, from Canada to Florida and Mexico. How? Nobody is quite sure.

It is certainly not a cop-out to say there is much mystery in our lives. It is not an attempt to excuse our limited understanding of so much – not least the way the invisible world of abstractions and thoughts operate. It is, rather, to insist that the texture of life can only be grasped if we stand back and reflect and marvel at the timeless features we have been exploring, however superficially.

7 SCIENCE – a friend

Science is far from being a list of certainties about the physical world. For a start it is experimental, endlessly testing and retesting, challenging theoretical explanations in the light of experience, often setting up hypotheses to see how well they stand up to scrutiny. All science is provisional: its theories are only valid until disproved.

As such, science complements and underscores some of the mystery and uncertainty explored in nature.

However, this is not usually the way scientists are presented, which is more about apparent certainties. As with many areas of life, reputations are more likely to be built on certainties, not doubts or questions. In medical circles the patient who hears his or her doctor expressing uncertainty may well seek a medic who looks like knowing what the illness is.

We saw evidence of the power of supposed experts during the Covid pandemic. It was all too easy for frightened and confused politicians and public to put these experts on a pedestal.

A good way into grasping the essence of science is to consider the impact of quantum mechanics. In the last century quantum theory seems to have overturned many basic assumptions of Newtonian mechanics (the traditional way of doing science).

Here are some features of quantum mechanics:

Uncertainty of outcome
Human observation in itself can make a difference.
Matter is congealed energy.
Entangled atomic particles can communicate instantly across space-time.

Possibly the first two points are the most significant for our present purposes: the uncertainty principle and the observer effect.

The uncertainty principle tells us that the world is far less fixed and predetermined than conventional science would suggest. The physical world is dynamic.

The observer effect is, if anything, even more significant because it underlines the point that there is no totally objective picture of the world to be had, as discussed in the Introduction. The world is as much what we make of it as it is intrinsically. This of course is well enough understood in the conduct of surveys and questionnaires in the social sciences. There is always some reactivity when a person is asked a question or knows they are being observed. But it comes as a surprise to some that this seems also to be the case in sciences like physics. Quantum theory undermines the idea that the physical world exists objectively and independently of human observers.

Parallels have been suggested between the quantum state and what could be described as mysticism. For example, in both:

Language cannot properly describe what is going on.

Symbols rather than hard observable states play a crucial part.

Time loses its conventional relevance (eg in entanglement there is no time at all between what happens in one entangled state and the other), and similarly in mystical states mystics report a sense of timelessness or at least transcendence where time loses its relevance.

Participation and observation play a crucial part in both: mental and physical are intertwined.

So quantum theory not only contains within itself ideas which are helpful to the case being made here: that there is more to the world than the obvious things we think we see. It also is helpful in exemplifying the provisional nature of science: as noted earlier, even old fashioned science works according to one theory until a new paradigm comes along which fits better with experimental evidence.

The scientific method as traditionally understood with its emphasis on accuracy, rigour and repeatability rather excludes those aspects of human life which don't fit properly with that model – broadly the arts, humanities and social sciences. The challenge here is to recognise and manage the uncertainty. Quantum theory encourages this approach.

However, it would be silly to suppose that science in the form of chemistry, physics and biology couldn't deal with physical measurable things. How otherwise could we trust the design of an aircraft or bridge? But it cannot deal with beauty, love, right and wrong, meaning in life, consciousness, purpose, and so on. If we (rightly) say that science delivers great benefits for humankind (relief of suffering, food security, housing, physical comfort, etc) these benefits are not defined as such by the science. These judgements are outside the scientific remit. They lie in the realm of philosophy, and the humanities generally. They entail ethical value judgements which have a timeless quality to them.

So we might say Science, guided by quantum, and accepting of its limitations, reveals insights which are remarkably well aligned with the speculations of this book. It is our friend, not a foe. It is therefore not surprising to find scientists who are open to realities which lie beyond the physical.

For example, Albert Einstein found mystery in the fact that the human mind had the capacity to comprehend the world, and by extension the cosmos. He found the experience of the mystical, and the awe associated with it, the source and inspiration of all true science.

Science invites ever more questions with its associated research agendas. It seems that the more scientists find out, the more they want to know. Take Black Holes as an example. This term was first used in the 1960's, though the theoretical possibility of a star with a fiercely strong gravitational pull preventing light leaving had existed long before then. In the last 60 years all sorts of questions have been raised about Black Holes. In the 1970's black hole thermodynamics emerged as a study.

In recent years it has seemed likely that Black Holes can be entangled with each other, along the lines of quantum entanglement. The questions and possibilities keep coming.

So Science models the principle of unfolding development. There is always something further to explore. Something beyond.

But it also presumes something timeless: that there are laws in science which cannot change even if what we *think* are the laws must admit of uncertainty and be open to revision. We touch not exactly on the eternal, but on what gets close.

8 Everlasting LOVE

Love takes various forms – romantic love, love of other people, love of friends, love of family, plus love of pets or animals, or books or holidays, and so on. Love is often portrayed in a sexualised way – which is fine, provided it is recognised as only part of a bigger picture.

Genuine love wants the best for the other person. It seeks their fulfilment. At the same time, and presumably by consent, it seeks its own. It is about that further step on the ladder. A further step towards completion. A testament to what is beyond.

If we consider the love we presume we see in a wedding, where and what is it? It isn't in a particular place, or even inside the bride and groom's body. It isn't even "all around" as one well known song insists. It is an invisible abstraction derived from feelings/emotions, actions like kissing or holding, etc. Yet even these are themselves partly abstractions based on interpretations. It would be possible, for example, for a couple to go through something like a sham marriage or marriage of convenience for financial, residential, or other reasons, where love could be feigned.

But assuming the love is "real" it is not any the less real simply because it is invisible. In fact, the wedding couple might insist that their love is the most real and important part of their lives!

Many people in love may want to say that their love will last forever – a lifetime and perhaps beyond. In a Church wedding the couple will usually promise to stay together "until death do us part". Some couples will claim their love goes further. They will want to say their love goes beyond death. Thus a surviving partner might feel it would be a betrayal of that love to remarry, or even have another relationship, as we noted previously.

A wedding ring is usually exchanged as a token of eternal love. The ring goes round and round indefinitely.

In popular love songs there are very many statements to the effect that the couple's love will never end.

Love is all around
You know I love you, I always will
My mind's made up by the way that I feel
There's no beginning, there'll be no end

Everlasting love
Be a lasting part of everlasting love
Real love will last forever
Open up your eyes, then you'll realize here I stand
With my everlasting love

This love will last forever
Oh, oh, lifting you higher
Oh, oh, is all I desire
This love will last forever

Our love will last forever
But we can't let anything
Be stronger than our love
We have to be able to see
That with love and trust
We can always work things out
Baby, we'll be as one for eternity

In some cases someone is not sure whether the love will last forever, though they aspire to that and may believe it will.

Eternal flame
Close your eyes, give me your hand
Do you feel my heart beating?
Do you understand? Do you feel the same?
Am I only dreaming?
Or is this burning an eternal flame?

For some lovers the love seems to share in, or look forward to, a future state, a state of future perfection.

Cheek to cheek
Heaven, I'm in heaven
And my heart beats so that I can hardly speak
And I seem to find the happiness I seek
When we're out together, dancing cheek to cheek

The power of love
We're heading for something
Somewhere I've never been
Sometimes I am frightened
But I'm ready to learn
Of the power of love

Sometimes there is a proper appreciation of how people change, while recognising that the person (shall we say his/her soul or spirit or mind) is still a constant.

Cherish
The world is always changing
Nothing stays the same
But love will stand the test of time
The next life that we live in
Remains to be seen
Will you be by my side
I often pray before I lay down by your side
If you receive your calling before I awake
Could I make it through the night

9 Living creatively with DEATH

It is not surprising that many of us fear death. Death has probably taken loved ones from us. Death can take any one of us without warning. Death brings an end to the pleasures of this life. The closer you have been to someone who has died, the more it hurts.

Sometimes our fear is to do with the loss of a loved one. Sometimes we fear our own deaths. Often the fears run in parallel – as when the death of a friend or loved one triggers fears for our own mortality.

Some people protest that they don't want – or need – to think about death. Surely this should not be a focus for mindful living. They might say something like: 'there are plenty of happy things with my life for me to focus on, so why dwell on something as morbid as death?'

Here are at least two possible responses. Death is *an inevitable* part of living – even the happy things we enjoy, like the music of Michael Jackson or Amy Winehouse, are framed now in the knowledge that they have died. In some ways listening to their songs has become more poignant following their passing. Secondly, we misconceive death if we make it out to be a fearsome thing. We sometimes hear the expression: "a good death". It isn't possible to say this of every death (especially the death of a younger person), but it is something to which to aspire.

Could we reframe or rethink death to see it as part of the natural order of things – part of a natural life cycle, as considered previously in the nature discussion? And could an understanding of death actually help us live better? At the very least, could we learn to contain or manage our fears?

We should make the effort for others, if not for ourselves, as our example of how to live positively in the face of death can be a model for them.

Maybe we can think of death as part of the 'deal' of having life. If we love nature, even if sometimes it seems cruel, why not think of death as part of the natural world that we cherish?

Life is a series of changes and losses. Some losses are relatively trivial – like parting with a piece of furniture we no longer need. Others are more serious – like losing a job. But change and loss are an inevitable part of the 'deal'. We can choose to go with the flow or, like Miss Haversham in Dicken's "Great Expectations" who had been jilted on her wedding day and spent the rest of her days in her wedding dress sitting with her wedding cake, we try to hold back the clock. Assuming we would choose to go with the flow (no choice really!), not Miss Haversham, it would be good to remember we have had some limited experience of coping with change and managing losses.

It may be helpful to think of life as if we were all taking part in a play. It has a certain inevitability about it. Some might even say that everything in life was all mapped out – as in an actual play. For example, the Italian tenor Luciano Pavarotti believed he had been predestined for his role in life. Some might say that there was only one certain person in the world whom they should marry.

Others might accept that not everything is mapped out in advance. The only certainties are taxes and death! But whatever your belief, it can be of comfort (and perhaps entertaining!) to think of us all as coming on, and going off, the stage of time. As Shakespeare put it in "As you like it"

All the world's a stage, and all the men and women merely players. They have their exits and their entrances.

We are changing all the time. We don't see our faces changing in the mirror as we stare at ourselves, but we see the change over time in photographs. As the years go by our character and temperament change in the light of experience. If you go to an occasional works or school reunion you'll see the difference in people! They don't look quite the same, and they present themselves somewhat differently in the light of experience. We 'lose' one person to 'find' another. Of course, when we lose a loved one we don't actually find another living breathing human being! But we 'find' a new perspective on the lost life. We have memories to celebrate and perhaps embellish! We will live our lives in companionship with those memories.

Perhaps we fear physical pain while we are dying. However, we know that while death sometimes is drawn out and painful that is the exception, not the rule. In any case we can remind ourselves that physical pain would not be something new. We have experience of coping!

We often hear or read the expression: *Rest in Peace (RIP)*. Less common these days are the words: *PERSON'S NAME has fallen asleep*, or *NAME has gone to his/her rest*. These are very comforting sentiments, but they are more than nice phrases. Death IS like falling asleep. In death a person IS at rest. If someone has suffered a lot of pain or had a difficult or hard life it is reassuring to know that those times are over. One day each one of us will be at rest. Not so bad after all!

If death is inevitable there is no point fretting about it. There is the well known Serenity prayer: *Grant me the serenity to accept the things I cannot change, courage to change the things I can, and the wisdom to know the difference.*

Instead of fearing the inevitable, think of the way death encourages us to make the best use of the time that we have left. The 80 year old film director, Martin Sorsese, said in a recent Sunday Times interview: "At this point in my life every moment is precious. Every frame of every picture is precious and every gesture..." Or, putting this slightly differently, but consistently with other things said in the interview, live each day in as kindly, generous and gentle way as possible, knowing this day could be your last.

Some of our fears when faced with the loss of a person may be connected to the questioning of our values or world view, or perhaps to do with anticipated changes in lifestyle or future relationships. Maybe we fear that we might cease to grieve the loss sufficiently. Maybe we fear life has lost any point or meaning.

Any such fears may seem reasonable enough, but they can be worked through, and partial solutions found. For example, perhaps it is true we might see less of some old friends, but that does not mean we can't make new ones.

But whatever the source of our fears, we should face them honestly, and it certainly helps to share our worries with others. Remember it is as well that we keep *some* respect or fear of death – otherwise we might live too dangerously!

We should expect to have some regrets in our later lives as we look back. We should also expect to feel disappointed that certain activities are no longer available to us. It would be amazing if this were not so! When Dame Judy Dench, aged 88, was asked whether she would like to play the part of Ophelia in "The Merchant of Venice" she replied "Oh God, I'd like another shot!" But sensibly she continued: "But of course it's too late. Does anyone want a really old Ophelia?"

She was thinking of her time in this life in a holistic organic way, as briefly discussed earlier when considering time. It flows. Equally she could be thinking of her lifetime as a sequence of seasons, as in the natural world. The key is to be able to relax into the flow of time.

If you think that there is only this life (ie no afterlife) you might fear that in death you would lose everything. But why be fearful? You didn't feel fear in the time before you were born, so why fear the time after you have died?

None of us can know for certain whether there is an afterlife. Many people – probably most – think that there is, and they would hope to meet up with loved ones again. They find comfort and reassurance in this belief, and many believe that they and others are helped thereby to live happier more fulfilled lives.

However, there are some who think that the idea of an afterlife is not attractive at all! One common objection would be that such a life would be incredibly monotonous and boring. Perhaps the experience of the elves in Tolkien's stories about Middle-Earth could be instructive. The elves are presented as immortal. They cannot die (except in special circumstances). Unsurprisingly, they grow weary of time and envy the life of humans where death brings things to an end.

However, we should distinguish between an existence that goes on forever and one that is timeless. Two words clarify the distinction. *Everlasting life* would be monotonous, but *eternal life* would be something different. The latter would suggest that the idea of repetition, with the associated monotony, simply wouldn't apply.

The concept of eternity can be surprisingly helpful in thinking about our lives here and now. The press of fitting everything into our lifespan looks silly when we imagine what eternity might be like. The philosopher Spinoza is famous for the phrase *sub specie aeternitatis* (under the aspect of eternity). So what if you have an extra 10 years more, or 10 years less, on your life? Would this make a difference to eternity?

If you are a believer in an afterlife, and draw comfort from this, you could argue that your belief is not just wishful thinking, or a faith for wimps afraid to face the challenge of dying. That would be to miss a crucial point. To repeat the argument: we humans yearn for completion, for purposes to be fulfilled, for justice. We have this disposition, we might suppose, because we are made for some ultimate purpose and fulfilment.

It used to be an amusing objection to the idea of an afterlife to ask where all these billions and billions of souls could be housed. That objection is heard less frequently now, perhaps because we are used to the way vast masses of data can be compactly stored in one way or another – on 'the cloud' or in a memory stick for example. Storage space ceases to be a problem. (There is possibly more reason to be anxious that our personal data is *too easily* stored without limit on time, so that things written or said at one point in one's life can return to haunt one at a later stage.)

A soul or spirit would not of course be a piece of data. So it wouldn't need even electronic storage space. It wouldn't occupy any space at all! Like the abstractions we have previously considered, it is not a physical thing. Storage space is not relevant!

All religions teach that there is a future life, as we shall see in the next chapter, so if you have a religious faith you will probably believe that death is not the end. Even if you have only a loose religious attachment you may still quite reasonably suppose that the insights of religion generally reflect a more fundamental human grasp on an unseen reality. But leaving religion aside for the moment, there are plenty of people whose spirituality includes a belief in survival beyond death, or who find there is evidence for such a belief. For example, they find the testimony of those who have claimed to have a Near Death Experience (when they have seemingly died but are resuscitated and believe they have had an out-of-body experience) convincing. Others are persuaded by the evidence of psychics and mediums. Others just sense that people live on in some form.

But none of this is proof in a scientific sense – at least that is what most independent researchers would say on the basis of what is known to date. But conventional science should not necessarily have the last word anyway. In fact, like so much else in life – relationships, the arts and the humanities, for example – it only tells a fraction of the full story.

A very recent book* written by experts in their respective fields (psychiatry, the nature of consciousness, philosophy, etc), committed to as objective analysis of data as possible, argues that the survival of a personal consciousness is the most natural and plausible explanation for all the findings and evidence we have available. To believe otherwise would be to swallow much unlikely theory, is the argument.

Personally, I find it easy enough to accept that there are spiritual powers, and that we all have a spiritual side to our human existence which cannot be lost. In the same way as in the physical world an atom is never lost (though it can be transformed) why

---

*2022 Science of life after death by A Moreira-Almeida, M de Abreu Costa, H Schubert Coelho. ISBN 978-3-031-06056-4

not expect the same in the spirit world? Perhaps you prefer to stick with the idea of personal consciousness, or perhaps personal energy, rather than spirit. But the argument remains the same: we don't expect a personal consciousness/spirit/energy to simply disappear when someone dies. Change – Yes. Annihilation – No. There is a parallel, we might suppose, with enduring unseen realities such as mathematical rules or core ethical principles which each can impact our lives in various ways.

There are very many hints of a timeless dimension beyond the physical world, as we have seen many times in previous chapters. Our survival beyond physical death may be more to do with becoming part of that timeless dimension than continuing the sort of earth-based lifestyle we are accustomed to.

Once we attempt to try to speculatively leave our familiar world of time and space we can easily lose our bearings and fumble for ways of thinking or talking about how we could exist. Religious pictures of heaven or paradise are creative – perhaps inspired – attempts to bridge the conceptual gap. At the very least the beauty they depict in itself speaks of eternal things. The art aspires to articulate something which is beyond understanding, and that very aspiration is testimony to something deep in the human psyche.

Even if the possibility of an afterlife in any form seems unlikely to you, there are still realities from a life which carry forward. We will live on through other people! We speak of ripples from a person's life. These have an enduring effect, though as time goes by those consequences become harder to see or quantify. The effects are most obvious if you have children. You can reasonably calculate that if you have 2 children and they in turn as adults average 2 children, and so on, then in 300 years there will be up to 1000 people alive who are your descendants! Those people would never have seen the light of day without your intervention! (These are gross speculative approximations of course. At the present time in the UK the average number of children born to a couple is slightly less than 2.)

But leaving children aside, if you take the influence one person has on countless others in a lifetime, and the way those influences will be played out in the lives of others and future generations, you have a similar sort of inverted pyramid to show the widening and timeless effect of the ripples.

So take heart if you are fearful of death. You are not alone! Others share your fears to a greater or lesser extent, even if they prefer not to talk about it. A thoughtful mindful approach, as discussed above, will pay dividends. Some children fear a bogeyman hiding under their bed. The solution might be to take a torch, crouch down on the floor and shine it in the darkness under the bed to dispel the fear! If you fear the bogeyman of death, get out your torch!

But let's not dwell on fear! Think rather of new horizons! After Tina Turner died in Spring 2023 Oprah Winfrey was quoted as saying: *She (Tina Turner) once said to me that when her time came to leave this earth she would not be afraid, but excited and curious...* Wouldn't it be wonderful if each of us could share Tina's sense of anticipation?

For those left behind, now in mourning, we try to find comfort where we can. Our grief is proportional to our love – and that in itself speaks of eternal things. Although the following quote from Shakespeare's Romeo and Juliet is here being taken out of context, it captures the essence of how a parting could be both sad and happy – a truly bitter-sweet moment. The sad loss of a loved one could be a measure of the love which had been shared so joyfully.

Parting is such sweet sorrow.

But we can see a further application. In the play Juliet was actually speaking of a very temporary overnight parting from Romeo, and the sweetness was the anticipation of being with him again in the morning. Could it be in the same way that the possibility of a future afterlife reunion with a loved one gives the parting a certain sweetness?

10 Some insights from RELIGION

In the earlier discussion of ritual we noted that at least some of the rituals associated with religion are trying to enact or convey a timeless dimension.

The Christian celebration of The Lord's Supper (the Eucharist, Holy Communion, Mass) is more than a memorial meal in many traditions. For believers it captures an eternal truth: that they can share in the ongoing merits of Jesus' death on the Cross by eating bread and drinking wine specially consecrated for the purpose.

There is a comparable enactment in the Jewish celebration of the Sabbath. This recalls God's goodness in the creation of the world, and his ongoing role in providing for his people. The Sabbath Candles are lit and bread and wine are shared.

In Sikhism the worship in the Gurdwara (Temple) has a focus on the holy scriptures, the Guru Granth Sahib, honoured as if it were itself a holy person or prophet. The believer through devotion to the Scriptures enters a divine timeless realm. The Zoroastrians believe that drinking a sacred liquor called 'haoma' confers immortality on the worshipper.

The religious quest is, generally speaking, about finding a deeper timeless meaning to life while still inevitably living in a way that is bounded by space and time. That timeless meaning believers would say comes to them now in fleeting incomplete ways. There is a sense of something to feel or experience now which heralds a fuller existence in a mystical future.

Typically that future is depicted as a state of joy or suffering depending on the judgement passed after death on life lived here on earth. Traditional Christian terminology is heaven and hell. These are paralleled in Islam with the terms Jannah and Jahannam. Buddhism and Hinduism both believe in a succession of reincarnations or rebirths — again determined by the kind of life a person had previously led. The ultimate goal is to reach Nirvana or Moksha.

Although there may be reference to time periods in the afterlife (eg a reincarnation would be for a particular period of time, and in the Roman Catholic and Islamic doctrine of Purgatory there is believed to be a period of purification and reform before entering heaven) the ultimate goal is a form of eternal or timeless existence with the divine. Believers in the existence of hell would say that for some there could be eternal pain and punishment.

Of course, the existence of religious belief proves nothing in itself. However, it is suggestive of some universal feature of human experience: the quest for a further dimension where the limits of time and space would not apply, a belief that the material world is passing and incomplete, a search for transcendence. There appears to be a human capacity or potential for religious belief which will take shape in different cultures influenced to a greater or lesser extent by a range of social, economic and geographical factors. We humans are made in a certain way. We seek purposes and fulfilment beyond the here and now.

There are further ways in which we can learn from religious practice. Most religions appear to believe that there are timeless forces operating in the world. The forces of good and evil would be good examples (we have previously considered the implications of our sense of right and wrong). You don't necessarily have to think there is a person called 'The Devil' or 'Satan' to believe in the power of evil. Or think that good acts must necessarily be inspired by a divine being. But you can see how religious belief can grow out of convictions about what is right and wrong, and can help sustain such convictions.

The experience of religious people of all faiths is that there are spiritual powers at work. In Judaism, Christianity and Islam some of the powers may be called angels. They are usually pictured as existing timelessly praising God, and occasionally intervening in human affairs. For example, the prophet Muhammad saw the Archangel Gabriel appear before him. In the Christian story Gabriel appeared to Mary to tell her she would be having a baby, and angels sang at Jesus' birth. In Shinto there are supernatural spirits which operationalise the forces of nature and are found in various places such as mountains or animals, and exercise power over human life.

We might sensibly ask: If many people (a majority in the world we might suppose) believe there really is some way in which a supreme being, or supreme beings, perhaps through angels and spirits, can influence human life, does this not suggest that the idea of such influences is not entirely far-fetched? Ben Fogle the television presenter whose programmes focus on remote locations finds continuing spiritual and religious power in the landscape and atmosphere of particular places, such as the Isle of Skye. Or perhaps you think we must dismiss the idea of spiritual or unseen influences as pure superstition?

But if you share Ben Fogle's belief that there is a timeless aspect to the power of places and cultural experiences — and extend that to music or art or moral virtue — then we are constantly touched by timeless forces and powers. We have direct experience of them, and thus of timeless entities or beings. In one sense this must be true: mathematical truths exert power over us as we saw in chapter 1. You can't make 2+2=5, however hard you try!

Not all such powers, however, might work for human flourishing. The powers of racism or nationalism, for example, are all around us. They might be driving human destiny in subtle subversive ways that few have recognised.

The power of a particular place may seem negative. An interesting illustration of this is the way a house where a suicide or murder has taken place will often have a lower value.

According to legal opinion in the UK failure to disclose such a past event (if known, of course) to a potential purchaser would give that purchaser a claim against the vendor. In some American states any previous death in a house must be disclosed to a purchaser.

What are we to make of this? Surely that at least a minority of people believe that a building can retain some sort of enduring memory of a negative event which could have a baleful influence on future people living there.

While a number of commentators have rightly drawn attention to the negative influences of religion, it may nevertheless, in one form or another, have a place in human experience as providing the ultimate stage of fulfilment. It makes sense of the intuitions we have been discussing previously by giving a structure, even if only in story-like form, for belief. Religion also provides a community framework in which that belief can be nurtured.

Intuitions about love – especially that it has an eternal aspect – make more sense when thought of as belonging to a supreme figure or spirit-power which some will choose to call God. It is not unreasonable to suppose that humans are created to an extent in the image of this supreme figure, and that that status takes precedence over their physical biology. They quite naturally would hope for a closer relationship with the supreme figure in an afterlife. Their spiritual and moral capacities would remain unfulfilled if death were simply the end.

Similarly, in so far as humans are social by nature, and seek fulfilment through fruitful relationships, the prospect of an afterlife where relationships are perfected makes good sense.

11 Last word echo

The singer-song writer Beyonce explored a number of human themes which had touched her lived experience in her 2022 Renaissance World Tour. While on the one hand the show speaks of aliveness and vitality, on the other it dwells on the way some aspects of our present culture (black, queer and trans life) are vulnerable. Even the world itself is portrayed as being in a precarious and possibly terminal state.

Yet the show extols the virtue of love and freedom – values which fit with what has been suggested in earlier chapters are perennial virtues. Interestingly, Beyonce emphasises release from the body. Her method is through music and movement, but equally we could see a more general application. She is putting in a plea for thinking beyond what is physical – beyond what we can see and touch.

During the show a quotation from Einstein may flash on the screen:

Imagination is more important than knowledge.

That statement captures the essence of what we have been discussing. Our knowledge is always limited, yet the capacity of our minds knows no bounds. Some of the imagery in the show is suggestive of life well beyond the box.

At the end of one performance Beyonce closed the show by telling her audience that she hoped they felt safe and loved. She encouraged everyone to hold a mental picture in their minds of how they felt at that moment – their emotions and perhaps how they were holding someone's hand or arm. "You can return to it anytime" she assured everyone.

"Yes," we might respond. "The products of our thinking and imagination indeed do have enduring qualities. They are indelible realities."
